P9-CAD-955

Disgusting Places

BY CONNIE COLWELL MILLER

Capstone
press

Mankato, Minnesota

Blazers is published by Capstone Press,
151 Good Counsel Drive, P.O. Box 669, Mankato, Minnesota 56002.
www.capstonepress.com

Copyright © 2007 by Capstone Press. All rights reserved.
No part of this publication may be reproduced in whole or in part, or stored in a retrieval
system, or transmitted in any form or by any means, electronic, mechanical,
photocopying, recording, or otherwise, without written permission of the publisher.
For information regarding permission, write to Capstone Press,
151 Good Counsel Drive, P.O. Box 669, Dept. R, Mankato, Minnesota 56002.
Printed in the United States of America

Library of Congress Cataloging-in-Publication Data
Miller, Connie Colwell, 1976–
    Disgusting places / by Connie Colwell Miller.
    p. cm.—(Blazers. That's disgusting!)
    Includes bibliographical references and index.
    ISBN-13: 978-0-7368-6801-3 (hardcover)
    ISBN-10: 0-7368-6801-1 (hardcover)
    ISBN-13: 978-0-7368-7879-1 (softcover pbk.)
    ISBN-10: 0-7368-7879-3 (softcover pbk)
    1. Bacteria—Juvenile literature. 2. Organic wastes—Juvenile literature. 3.
Hygiene—Juvenile literature. 4. Hazardous geographic environments—Juvenile
literature. I. Title. II. Series.
QR74.8.M55 2007
616.9'201—dc22   2006026491

Summary: Describes 10 disgusting places and what makes them gross.

Editorial Credits
Mandy Robbins, editor; Thomas Emery, designer; Bob Lentz, illustrator;
    Jo Miller, photo researcher

Photo Credits
Corbis, 6–7; Judy Griesedieck, 16–17; Richard Hamilton Smith, 20–21;
    Star Ledger/Patti Sapone, 22 (inset); Sygma/Pascal Le Segretain, 26–27;
    zefa/Mika, 9
Getty Images Inc./Iconica/Peter Cade, 9 (inset); Stone/Jeff Mermelstein, 28–29;
    Taxi/Jeff Sherman, cover; Rob Brimson, 13
PhotoEdit Inc./ David Young-Wolff, 14–15; Michael Newman, 4–5
Photo Researchers, Inc/Steve Gschmeissner, 15 (inset); Will & Deni McIntyre, 22–23
Shutterstock/R, 11 (inset)
SuperStock/age footstock, 25; Robert Huberman, 18–19
Visuals Unlimited/Dr. Dennis Kunkel, 11

1 2 3 4 5 6 12 11 10 09 08 07

Table of Contents

That's Disgusting!

Cats poop and pee in litter boxes. Owners scoop out the dirty litter.

The world has many places filled with garbage, germs, or fumes. Some places are easy to spot, and others are hidden. But they are all gross.

GROSS-O-METER

Use this meter to gauge how disgusting these places really are.

THAT'S DISGUSTING

Coal Mines

Digging in coal mines stirs up smelly fumes and thick black dust. People can die from breathing in coal dust for long periods of time.

GROSS-O-METER

SORT OF DISGUSTING

BLAZER FACT

In the 1800s, many men worked in coal mines. By the end of each day, they were covered in black coal dust.

When You Gotta Go

Even clean bathrooms are full of germs. Flushing toilets shoots out bits of waste too small to see. Not washing your hands can spread these germs and make people sick.

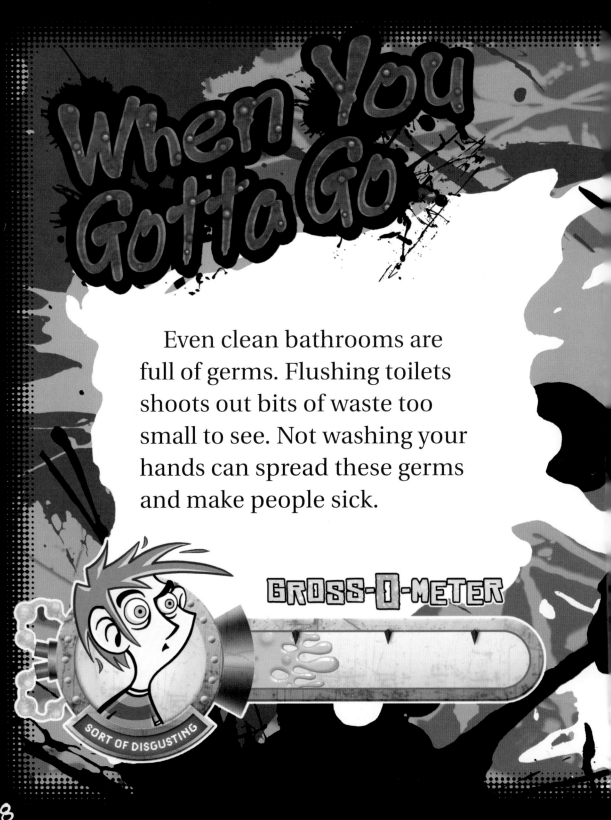

GROSS-O-METER

SORT OF DISGUSTING

BLAZER FACT

In your bathroom, germs often land on your toothbrush.

Cover your toothbrush!

The Kitchen Sink

The kitchen is even dirtier than the bathroom. More germs live in your sink and on sponges and dishcloths than on your toilet seat!

GROSS-O-METER

SORT OF DISGUSTING

Germs in a kitchen sink

Dirty water in a sink

The Sewer

Rivers of poop and pee flow under the streets. The sewers take water waste from toilets to treatment plants. People reuse the water after it is cleaned.

GROSS-O-METER

SORT OF DISGUSTING

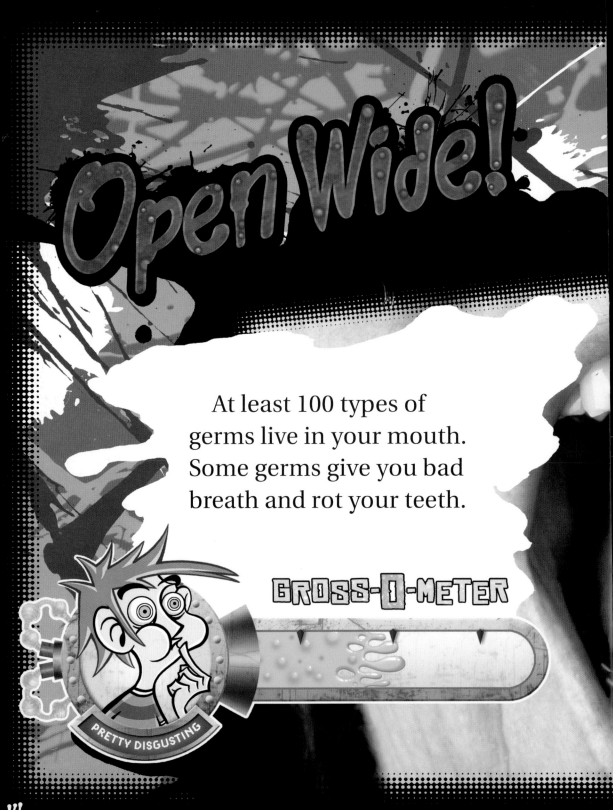

Open Wide!

At least 100 types of germs live in your mouth. Some germs give you bad breath and rot your teeth.

GROSS-O-METER

PRETTY DISGUSTING

Some scientists think that as many as 500 types of germs live in your mouth.

Germs on a human tongue

Smells Fishy

Dead fish pile up in fish canneries. A nasty stink fills the air as workers remove guts and bones. That job goes to you if you go fishing.

GROSS-O-METER

PRETTY DISGUSTING

To the Bat Cave

BLAZER FACT

Some people collect bat guano to use as fertilizer!

Bat caves are full of slimy bat poop called guano. Some caves have layers of guano that are more than 100 years old.

GROSS-O-METER

PRETTY DISGUSTING

Hog Farms

Hog poop piles up in pits beneath their pens. This poop turns into liquid that releases a smelly gas. The gas can make people sick.

GROSS-O-METER

PRETTY DISGUSTING

Taking Out the Trash

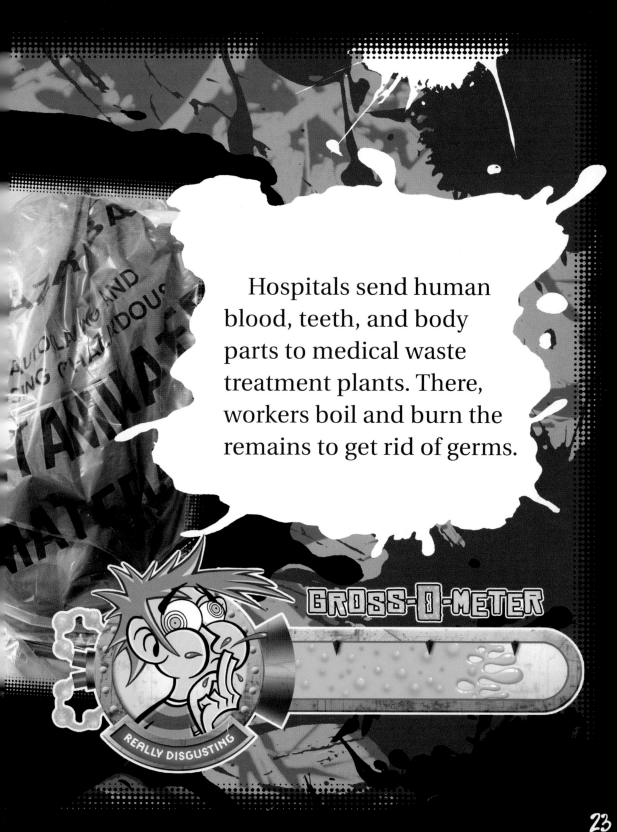

Hospitals send human blood, teeth, and body parts to medical waste treatment plants. There, workers boil and burn the remains to get rid of germs.

GROSS-O-METER

REALLY DISGUSTING

Cold Storage

Dead bodies are stored in morgues. Just like refrigerators keep food fresh, morgues are kept cold so the bodies don't rot.

GROSS-O-METER

REALLY DISGUSTING

BLAZER FACT

In some countries, bodies remain in morgues for more than a year!

Slaughterhouses

BLAZER FACT

Animal heads, bones, and fat are used in soaps, candles, and fuel.

Slaughterhouses smell like raw meat. White cutting boards turn pink as workers chop up slabs of meat.

GROSS-O-METER

REALLY DISGUSTING

Down in the Dumps

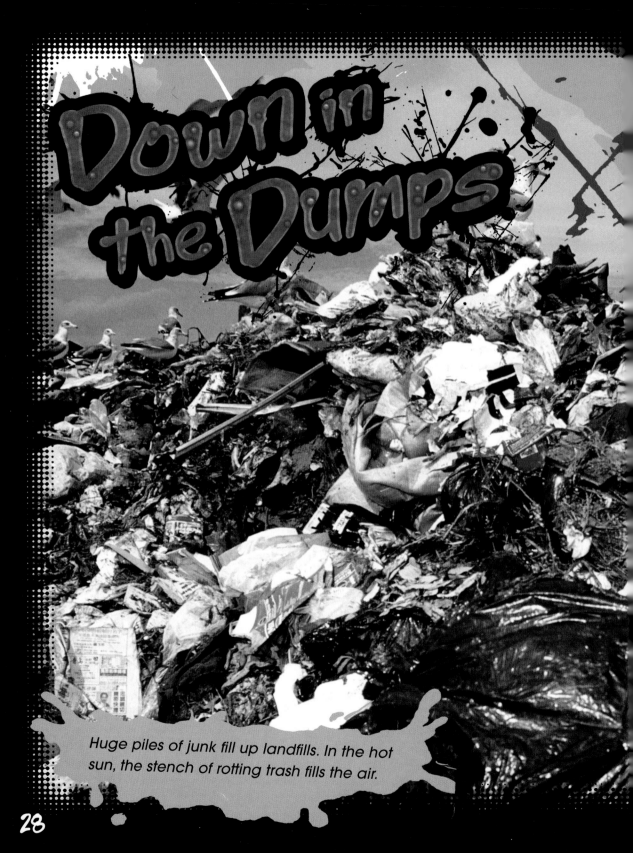

Huge piles of junk fill up landfills. In the hot sun, the stench of rotting trash fills the air.

Disgusting places are everywhere. Some you can avoid, like bat caves and morgues. Others are as close as your own mouth!

We made it through, and I have one thing to say. **That's disgusting!**

Glossary

fertilizer (FUR-tuh-lize-ur)—a substance used to make plants grow better

fume (FYOOM)—unpleasant or harmful gas, smoke, or vapor given off by something burning or by chemicals

guano (GWAH-noh)—bat poop; guano is often used as fertilizer.

inhale (in-HAYL)—to breathe in

landfill (LAND-fill)—a place filled with garbage that is stacked and covered with earth

stench (STENCH)—a strong, unpleasant smell

Read More

Masoff, Joy. *Oh, Yuck! The Encyclopedia of Everything Nasty.* New York: Workman, 2000.

Szpirglas, Jeff. *Gross Universe: Your Guide to All Disgusting Things Under the Sun.* Toronto: Maple Tree Press, 2004.

Internet Sites

FactHound offers a safe, fun way to find Internet sites related to this book. All of the sites on FactHound have been researched by our staff.

Here's how:

1. Visit *www.facthound.com*

2. Choose your grade level.

3. Type in this book ID **0736868011** for age-appropriate sites. You may also browse subjects by clicking on letters, or by clicking on pictures and words.

4. Click on the **Fetch It** button.

FactHound will fetch the best sites for you!

Index